Written by Sherria L. Elliott

Illustrated by Sasha Moore

For information regarding permission, write to:
4Elliott Publishing, Inc.
Attention: Permissions Department
16759 SW 16th St, Pembroke Pines, FL 33027
Email to: 4Elliottpublishing@gmail.com or call: 786-277-2693
www.4Elliottpublishing.com

ISBN: 978-0-9846963-4-5

Library of congress cataloging Publication Data Pending
Manufactured in the United States of America.

This edition of the "But Mommy It's Not Fair!" series is dedicated not only to my daughter Sheterria "Heaven" Elliott, but to my daughter She'riq "Khalani" Elliott, who was also born with Albinism.

She'riq, your birth was a pivotal moment in Sheterria's life, where she was able to realize, indeed, she was not alone! Going through life up until the point of your birth for Sheterria was difficult because she had no one to relate to. The look of pure love, and admiration she had once she laid eyes on you was breathtaking, but the bond you two now share is priceless!

I love and cherish you both, as you two were clearly sent from "HEAVEN", both your middle-names sake.

"Khalani "– means (sent from Heaven) in Hawaiian.

Love, Mom

This book belongs to:

_____

Heaven sat in the car, staring out the window. Her big brother Tee-Tee was taking her to school, but all she could think about was her mom who was taken to the hospital.

Her mom was about to give birth to Heaven's twin sister and brother, and Heaven really wanted to be there.

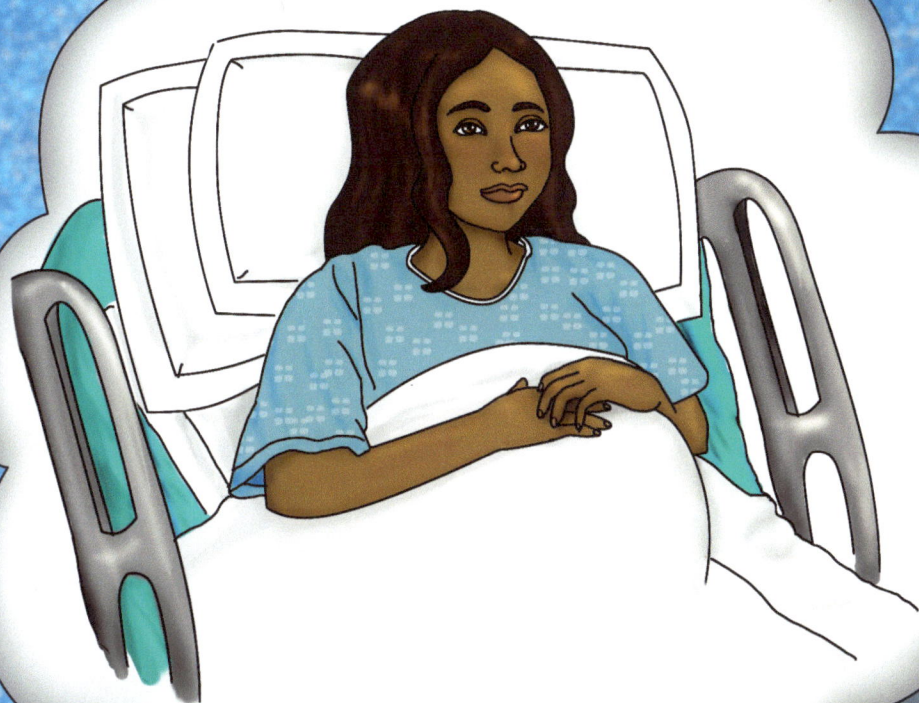

"But I don't want to go to school today!" she would say.

As they arrived at school, her big brother smiled and promised her that she was going to the hospital right after school. Heaven gave Tee-Tee a big hug and hurried to class.

Heaven could not get through the school day without worrying every minute about what was happening at the hospital. She had a secret wish and hoped it would come true!

All her life, Heaven felt she was alone because she was "different" than her family. Although she was given unconditional love and support from her family, she couldn't help feeling alone.

Heaven felt this way because she is an African American girl who is the only member in her family born with "Albinism." This is a genetic condition that leaves her with little color or no pigment in her hair, skin, and eyes. She is the only one in her family with pretty blonde hair, soft milky skin, and gorgeous grey eyes.

All Heaven could think of in school was about the birth of her twin siblings. But most important to Heaven was how they would look. What Heaven kept hidden in her thoughts was her secret wish that only she and her daddy knew.

Heaven prayed that one of her siblings would look just like her! She longed to have a sibling she could relate to. She prayed every day and hoped that her prayers would come true!

Finally, Heaven's dad came to pick her up from school. She could hardly get into the car before asking a million questions at once!

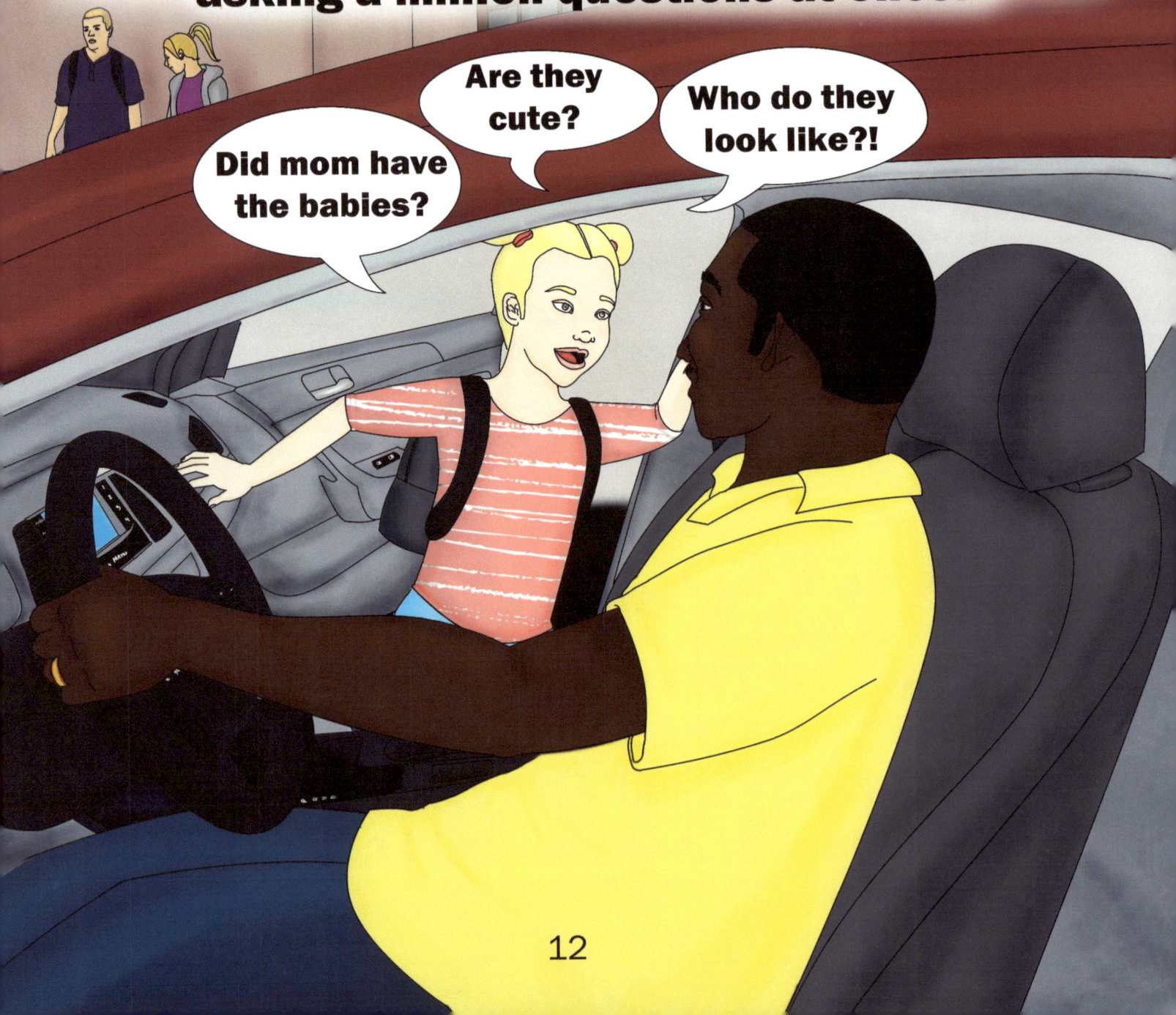

12

Heaven's dad knew the last question was the most important to her, because he shared Heaven's wish that at least one of the twins be born with Albinism as well. As her father, he knew there was a 75% chance it could happen, and he knew that it would really help Heaven in her self-discovery to fill that void of being "different."

 = 75%

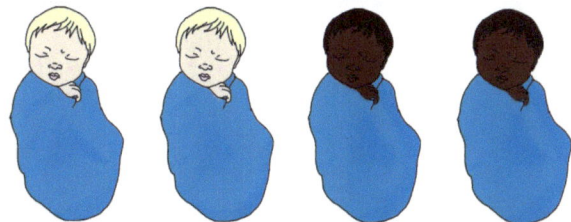 = 50%

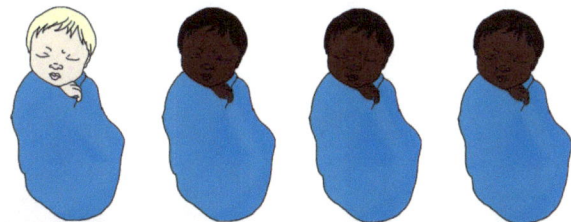 = 25%

 = 0%

13

Heaven's dad, Terry, could hardly wait to see the look on her face when she saw her new siblings. What he was not going to tell her was that her wish had come true! He wanted to see the look on her face when she discovered someone as breathtaking as her.

At the hospital, as Heaven prepared to see her twin brother and sister for the first time, all the nursing staff was anxious to see her reaction. They had been told of her secret wish and wanted to take part in this sure to be joyous moment.

All eyes were on Heaven as her mom brought the twins to her side. First there was her brother Te'riq, and she was amazed at how cute he was. But you could see a little flicker of disappointment that he was not born with Albinism.

16

But then, she saw her sister She'riq. Her hands went to her face in amazement and she let out the biggest scream saying, "She looks like me!" She looks like me!" and she started crying.

17

Everyone in the NICCU was so touched with emotion that they started crying as well.

Heaven could not believe her secret wish had just become a reality. She really had someone to relate to. Someone who was the very image of her beautiful self. All her prayers had been answered and she could see "she was not alone."

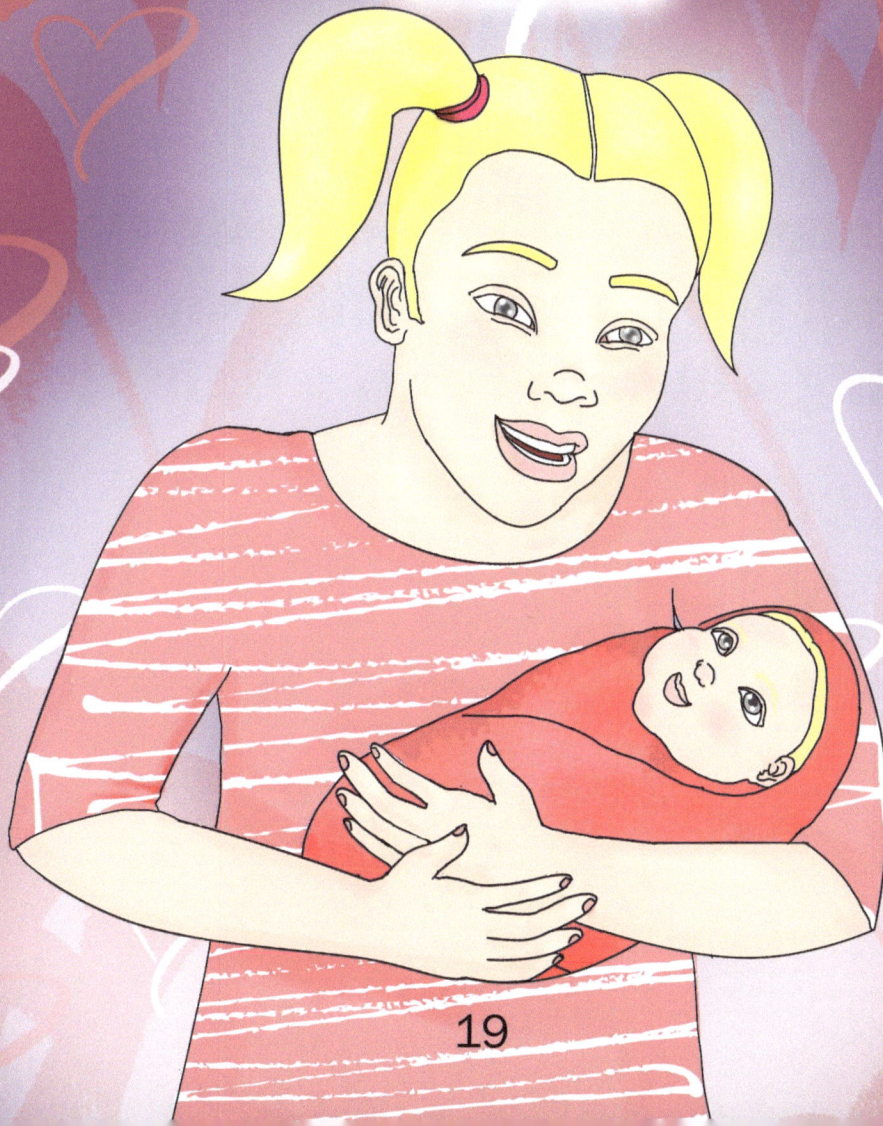

The End

Heaven's message is that sometimes you may feel alone, but if you're faithful, the right blessing will come at the right time.

Family Photobook

Family Photobook

Family Photobook

Family Photobook

www.ingramcontent.com/pod-product-compliance
Lightning Source LLC
Chambersburg PA
CBHW040024050426
42452CB00002B/117